Over the River
and Through the Wood

Over the River
and Through the Wood

by **Lydia Maria Child**

pictures by **Nadine Bernard Westcott**

HarperCollins*Publishers*

Over the river and through the wood,
To grandfather's house we go;

The horse knows the way
To carry the sleigh
Through the white and drifted snow.

Over the river and through the wood—
  Oh, how the wind does blow!
    It stings the toes
     And bites the nose,
   As over the ground we go.

Over the river and through the wood,
 To have a first-rate play.
  Hear the bells ring,
  Ting-a-ling-ding!
 Hurrah for Thanksgiving Day!

Over the river and through the wood,
Trot fast, my dapple-gray!
Spring over the ground
Like a hunting-hound!
For this is Thanksgiving Day!

Over the river and through the wood,
  And straight through the barnyard gate.
    We seem to go
    Extremely slow—
  It is so hard to wait!

Over the river and through the wood—
Now grandmother's cap I spy!

Hurrah for the fun!

Is the pudding done?
Hurrah for the pumpkin-pie!

Over the River
and Through the Wood

With galloping motion

arr. Ray Kimmelman

O - ver the ri - ver and | through the wood, To | grand - fa - ther's house   we
O - ver the ri - ver and | through the wood, To | have _____ a   first - rate
O - ver the ri - ver and | through the wood, And | straight through the   barn - yard

go; _____ The | horse knows the way   To | car - ry the sleigh   Through the
play. _____ | Hear the bells ring, _____ | "Ting- a - ling- ding!"   Hur -
gate. _____ | We seem to go _____ | Ex - treme- ly slow—   It _____

D7	G7	C	

white __ and drift - ed | snow. _____ | O-ver the ri-ver and | through the wood— Oh,
rah for Thanks-giv - ing | Day! _____ | O-ver the ri-ver and | through the wood, Trot
is __ so hard to | wait! _____ | O-ver the ri-ver and | through the wood— Now

F	C	F	

how _____ the wind does | blow! _____ It | stings __ the toes | And __
fast, _____ my dap - ple - | gray! __ Spring | o - ver the ground | Like a
grand-mo-ther's cap I | spy! _____ Hur- | rah for the fun! | Is the

C	Am	C	G7	C

bites the nose, | As | o - ver the ground we | go.
hunt - ing-hound! | For | this is Thanks-giv - ing | Day!
pud - ding done? | Hur- | rah for the pump - kin- | pie!

For Jenny R.

The poem "Over the River and Through the Wood" was originally
titled "A Boy's Thanksgiving Day," published in 1844 in
Flowers for Children by Lydia Maria Child.

Over the River and Through the Wood
Text by Lydia Maria Child
Illustrations copyright © 1993 by Nadine Bernard Westcott
Printed in the U.S.A. All rights reserved.
Music copying and caligraphy by Christina T. Davidson
Typography by Michele Chism
1 2 3 4 5 6 7 8 9 10 ❖
First Edition

Library of Congress Cataloging-in-Publication Data
Child, Lydia Maria Francis, 1802–1880.
    [Boy's Thanksgiving Day]
    Over the river and through the wood / by Lydia Maria Child ; pictures by
Nadine Bernard Westcott.
        p.   cm.
    Summary: An illustrated version of the well-known text describing the
joys of a Thanksgiving visit to grandmother's house.
    ISBN 0-06-021303-5. — ISBN 0-06-021304-3 (lib. bdg.)
    1. Children's songs—Texts.   [1. Thanksgiving Day—Songs and music.
2. Songs.]   I. Westcott, Nadine Bernard, ill.   II. Title.
PZ8.3.C4335Ov   1992   92-14979
782.4216'0268—dc20   CIP
                                                                  AC